REDISCOVER CHRISTMAS

A 26 DAY DEVOTIONAL

NATHAN MARSH

Contents

For every heart that finds it difficult to
celebrate this season—
may you find comfort here.
This is for you.

INTRODUCTION

*C*hristmas often arrives in a blur. There are lights to hang, gifts to wrap, events to attend, and meals to plan. Amid all the activity, it's easy to miss the wonder—easy to forget the why behind the season. That's where *Advent* comes in.

The word *Advent* means "coming" or "arrival." For centuries, Christians around the world have observed the four weeks leading up to Christmas as a sacred season of anticipation. It's a time to prepare our hearts for the arrival of Jesus—not just as a baby in a manger, but as our Savior, Redeemer, and returning King.

Advent isn't about adding one more thing to your already busy to-do list. It's an invitation to slow down, reflect, and rediscover. It's about waiting with hope, watching with wonder, and remembering that God stepped into our world, and is still stepping into our lives today.

That's the heart behind this *Rediscover Christmas devotional.* Over these next 26 days, we'll journey together through Scripture, reflection, prayer, and intentional action. Each day invites you to rediscover something essential to this season and your faith.

Each day also includes a daily journaling prompt. I want to encourage you to grab a journal or, if you prefer, open a notes app on your device. Taking time to write will help

you engage more deeply and notice how God is moving in your life throughout this season.

Whether you've walked through many Advents before or this is your first time pausing to reflect in this way, this devotional is for you. Come as you are—tired or hopeful, grieving or joyful, questioning or certain. **The story of Christmas is for *all* of us.**

Thank you for joining me on this journey. I'm truly grateful to walk through this season with you, and I'm expectant about what God is doing—and what God continues to do—in your life. May you rediscover the wonder, beauty, and nearness of Christ this Christmas.

REDISCOVER HOPE

Day

Scripture

The people walking in darkness have seen a great light; on those living in the land of deep darkness a light has dawned.
- Isaiah 9:2

1

Reflection

*I*t was a night like any other. The shepherds were doing what they always did: keeping watch under a cold, starlit sky. There was no indication that anything would be different, but then, without warning, Heaven broke into Earth. Light pierced the darkness. An angel appeared and declared a message that would echo across eternity: "Today, in the town of David, a Savior has been born to you."

Hope had arrived. But the shepherds

didn't just stumble upon it. Hope sought *them* out.

That's the thing about hope—it often shows up when we least expect it, and sometimes when we need it the most. It happens in the moments we're convinced nothing will ever change. It also happens in the silence that feels unending. It penetrates the weariness that settles into our bones.

Many of us step into this Advent season with the weight of unmet expectations, buried grief, or lingering questions. We carry around silent prayers and hidden doubts. If we're honest, Christmas can sometimes magnify those tensions, making us wonder if the light is still shining at all.

Isaiah had the boldness to proclaim light was coming while the world was still cloaked in darkness. He dared to believe that a better day was on the horizon, not because circumstances looked hopeful, but because God had promised it.

That's the essence of Biblical hope. It's not blind optimism or forced cheerfulness. It's the deep, settled confidence that the God who came *will* come again. It also declares that God, who moved in the past, is still moving in our present.

Advent is more than a countdown to Christmas; it's a season of waiting with expectation. It invites us to look back at the manger and look forward to the return of the King. It invites us to live in the middle of the already and the not yet—with hearts anchored in hope.

So today, lift your eyes. The same God who sent light to a group of shepherds on an ordinary night still sends light to you. Not because you've figured it all out or because you feel especially faithful, but because you are loved, seen, and Jesus is still Emmanuel—God with us.

Let this Advent be a journey of rediscovery and may it begin here—with hope.

Prayer

Jesus, You are my hope. In a world full of uncertainty and darkness, You shine with a light that never fades. Help me rediscover what it means to live with expectant faith. Even when I don't see it, help me trust that You are working. Help me find hope in You again. Amen.

Today's Journaling Prompt

Candles have long been a symbol of hope. Light a candle this evening and sit quietly for five minutes. As you watch the flame, reflect on areas in your life where you feel a need for hope. Write a short prayer in your journal asking Jesus to shine His light in those places. Then spend time in prayer, thanking Him for being your steady source of hope, even in the waiting.

REDISCOVER WAITING

Scripture

I wait for the Lord, my whole being waits, and in his word I put my hope.
- Psalm 130:5

Reflection

Day

2

*W*aiting is not easy. Whether it's sitting in traffic, standing in a long checkout line, or waiting on God to answer a prayer, none of us enjoys it. We live in a world that values speed, instant answers, and immediate results. But the story of Christmas is, at its heart, a story of waiting.

God's people had waited for generations—hundreds of years—for the promised Messiah. Prophets had spoken, promises had been made, but the silence stretched on. Still, a faithful remnant waited, clinging to the hope that God had not forgotten them.

Then one day, in a quiet town, through an unlikely young woman, a baby's cry broke the silence.

God's timing is rarely our timing, but His delays are never without purpose.

When we learn to wait well, something shifts in us. We begin to pay attention. We start looking for God's presence in the in-between. Waiting slows us down, refines our focus, and prepares our hearts.

Maybe you're in a season of waiting right now—waiting for healing, direction, reconciliation, or peace to return to your soul. Advent reminds us that waiting is not wasted when it's rooted in trust.

God is at work in the waiting, not far off, closer than you think, and weaving together a story bigger than what you see. The silence isn't the end of the story—it's the space before the miracle.

Prayer

Lord, teach me to wait with hope. In moments where I feel restless or forgotten, help me remember that You are faithful. Give me patience in the process and peace in the waiting. Let this season of Advent shape my heart to trust in Your perfect timing. Amen.

Today's Journaling Prompt

Write down one area of your life where you're currently waiting on God. Offer it in prayer. Ask God to help you grow in trust as you wait. Then, each day this week, thank God for being at work—even if you can't yet see the outcome.

REDISCOVER WONDER

Scripture

**And all who heard it were amazed at what the shepherds said to them.
- Luke 2:18**

Reflection

Day

3

Children rarely need help finding wonder. They're amazed by the sparkle of lights, the rustle of wrapping paper, and the sound of Christmas music. They stop to look at things we've grown used to.

They ask questions we've stopped asking.

Somewhere along the way, we adults lose our sense of awe. Life gets busy. Troubles mount. We grow more cynical than curious.

But the Christmas story is full of wonder.

A virgin conceives. Angels fill the night sky with song. Shepherds abandon their flocks to find a baby wrapped in cloths. Wise men travel for miles, guided by a star. At the center of it all—a tiny baby who is also the King of Kings and Lord of Lords.

Wonder is what happens when the soul wakes up to the presence of God.

If you've felt jaded or numb, if the season feels more like stress than joy, maybe what you need is to pause long enough to be amazed again. Step outside at night and look at the stars. Read the story of Jesus' birth like it's your first time. Ask God to open your eyes and soften your heart.

Because wonder isn't something you force—it's something you notice.

Prayer

God, awaken wonder in me again. Help me slow down and see the beauty of what You've done. Let me rediscover the awe of Emmanuel—God with us. May my heart be filled with joyful wonder this season. Amen.

Today's Journaling Prompt

Find one thing today that amazes you—a sunset, a smile, a song. Write it down or draw a picture in your journal and pause to thank God for it. Then write down *three things* you see or experience that remind you of God's nearness.

REDISCOVER PEACE

Scripture

**Glory to God in the highest heaven, and on earth peace to those on whom his favor rests.
- Luke 2:14**

Reflection

Day

4

*W*e all long for peace, but in a world filled with noise, conflict, and worry, peace can feel hard to find. Even in this season meant to celebrate peace, our hearts are often anything but peaceful.

Christmas reminds us that peace is not the absence of problems—it's the presence of a Person.

When the angels announced peace on Earth, they weren't promising a world without war or pain. They were proclaiming that the Prince of Peace had come. The One who could bring rest to our anxious hearts and calm to our weary souls had arrived.

And God still does.

Peace doesn't always mean everything is perfect. It means you're not alone. It means you have a refuge in the storm, an anchor when the waves rise. It means you can be still, even when the world is spinning.

Jesus came not just to bring peace to the world but to bring peace *within* you.

Today, if your thoughts are racing or your heart is heavy, take a moment to pause. Breathe. Remember that peace is a Person— and His name is Jesus. You don't have to carry everything on your own. Let Him hold you.

Prayer

Jesus, You are my peace. In the chaos of this world and the swirl of this season, help me rest in You. Quiet my heart. Settle my thoughts. Fill me with the kind of peace that only You can give. Amen.

Today's Journaling Prompt

Take ten slow, deep breaths and invite Jesus into your heart and mind. As you exhale, silently pray, "Jesus, be my peace." Then write about one place in your life where you need His peace today. After you write this down, search God's Word for promises that bring calm to the chaos of the situation you mentioned. Write down those Scripture references.

REDISCOVER JOY

Scripture

Do not be afraid. I bring you good news that will cause great joy for all the people. - Luke 2:10

Reflection

Day

5

*J*oy is not the same as happiness. Happiness depends on circumstances—on things going well, feeling good, or falling into place. But joy runs deeper. Joy is rooted in something unshakable, something eternal.

The angel's announcement to the shepherds was clear: this was "good news that will cause great joy."

Not just temporary happiness. Not momentary excitement. But joy that breaks through fear, uncertainty, and hardship. The kind of joy that lives even in the middle of tears. That's the joy Jesus brings.

It's joy that doesn't ignore the pain—but shines through it. It's the deep assurance that God is with us, God is for us, and God is at work—even in the mess. Joy isn't loud or showy—it can be quiet, even hidden. But it's there, like an ember burning beneath the ashes, ready to glow again.

This joy doesn't fade with the season. It's not tied to twinkling lights or gifts under the tree. It's anchored in a Savior who came near and never left. In Jesus, we discover a joy that can sit with sorrow and still sing. A joy that doesn't depend on what's around us, but on the One who dwells within us.

You may not feel joyful today, but that doesn't mean joy is gone. Sometimes, joy is a quiet strength. A soft song in the storm. A flicker of light in the dark. You can hold both sorrow and joy—and Jesus meets you in both.

So go ahead—laugh, smile, sing, or simply whisper thanks. **The joy of the Lord is your strength.** Even now. Especially now.

Prayer

Father, thank You for joy that goes deeper than my circumstances. Help me rediscover the joy of Your presence. Teach me to choose joy, even when it's hard. Let Your joy be my strength today. Amen.

Today's Journaling Prompt

Do one thing today that brings you joy—big or small. Here are some possibilities. Take a walk, color, paint, pursue a hobby, or spend quality time with a family member. Then write a short list of five things you're grateful for. Thank God for these in prayer and let gratitude stir joy in your soul.

REDISCOVER GRACE

Day

Scripture

For it is by grace you have been saved, through faith—and this is not from yourselves, it is the gift of God - Ephesians 2:8

6

Reflection

*G*race is hard to accept. We live in a world built on merit—where you get what you earn. Good grades get rewards. Hard work gets promotions. Niceness often comes with conditions. But grace isn't like that. It's unearned, undeserved, and often unbelievable, especially when we know the depths of our own failures.

This is what makes grace so disruptive. It doesn't play by the rules we're used to. When we mess up, we expect punishment. When we fall short, we brace for disappointment.

However, grace shows up with open arms, not a pointed finger. Christmas itself is a divine declaration of this truth. A perfect Savior came for imperfect people. A King born not in a palace, but in a stable—for you, for me, for the unworthy.

We struggle to believe it because we know ourselves too well. We replay the mistakes, carry the guilt, nurse the shame. We wonder if grace really applies to *that* part of our story—the messy part, the hidden part, the part we hope no one ever sees. **But grace goes there.** It meets us not just at our best, but precisely at our worst.

If grace feels too good to be true, you're starting to understand it. It's supposed to undo you. It's supposed to leave you speechless, and still, God wants you to receive it anyway. Let grace wash over your regrets and silence the inner critic. Let it fill you with awe that such love would dare draw near. Grace isn't a reward for the righteous—it's a gift for the guilty. And it is yours today.

God didn't send Jesus to applaud our efforts or reward our goodness—He sent Him to rescue us in our weakness. That's what makes grace so powerful. In our striving, our stumbling, our secret shame, grace breaks in with a better word: *enough*. Enough striving. Enough self-condemnation. Enough pretending and performing. Jesus came not to help you earn grace but to be grace for you.

This Christmas season, let yourself be stunned again by grace. Don't rush past it. Don't try to deserve it. Just sit with it. The same grace that brought salvation to a manger in Bethlehem is the same grace reaching for you now. No matter what you've done. No matter how far you've run. Grace has come—and it has your name on it.

Prayer

Lord, thank You for the grace I can never earn. Help me stop striving for approval and instead rest in Your love. Fill me with the wonder of Your mercy. Amen.

Today's Journaling Prompt

Write down at least one failure or regret. Cross it out, then write the word "GRACE" over it in big letters. Reflect on how God's love covers it completely.

REDISCOVER MERCY

Scripture

Because of the Lord's great love we are not consumed, for his compassions never fail. They are new every morning; great is your faithfulness.
- Lamentations 3:22-23

Day

7

Reflection

*M*ercy is one of the most beautiful and misunderstood gifts of God. It's more than a second chance—it's the consistent, undeserved kindness of God reaching into our lives again and again. It meets us at our lowest, embraces us in our mess, and gently lifts our eyes to hope. **Mercy is the love of God in motion.**

When the prophet Jeremiah wrote these verses, he was standing in the ruins of Jerusalem. Grief and sorrow were everywhere. And yet, amid despair, he declared something astonishing: God's mercy is *new every morning*. Not used up. Not recycled. New and fresh. Ready to meet the next failure or heartache with compassion and hope.

That's what makes mercy so powerful—it's not earned, and it doesn't expire. No matter what yesterday looked like, mercy meets us at the sunrise. It doesn't wait for us to get it all together. It even runs to us in the middle of our chaos.

Christmas tells this same story. Jesus didn't wait for a perfect world to arrive. He came into a messy stable, into a hurting humanity, into our need. His entire life was marked by mercy—toward lepers, tax collectors, the outcast, and the ashamed. He didn't turn away from their brokenness. He stepped into it, and He still does.

When you feel weighed down by guilt, fear, or regret, remember: His mercy is louder than your shame. Stronger than your failure. More faithful than your wandering heart. Let that mercy wash over you today.

Prayer

God, thank You that Your mercies for my life are new today. Even when I fall, You lift me. Even when I run, You welcome me home. Teach me to live in the freedom of Your mercy. Amen.

Today's Journaling Prompt

Start by identifying an area in your life where you need God's mercy. It could be a moment of failure, a struggle with guilt, or an area where you need healing. Acknowledge that God's mercy is waiting to meet you there, fresh and new, just as it does every morning.

One day later, take time to reflect: How did God's mercy show up in your life today? Were there moments where you felt His embrace, His compassion, or His guidance? Write about those experiences and thank God for His unwavering, faithful mercy.

REDISCOVER SIMPLICITY

Scripture

**And what does
the Lord require of you? To act
justly and to love mercy and to
walk humbly with your God.
- Micah 6:8**

Reflection

Day

8

*T*he first Christmas wasn't complicated. There were no glittering trees, no endless to-do lists, no perfectly curated Instagram posts. It was quiet, humble, and profoundly holy. A young couple, some rough-looking shepherds, and the cry of a baby in a borrowed manger—that was it. Yet in that simple setting, Heaven touched Earth.

We live in a world obsessed with more—more decorations, more events, more pressure to create the "perfect" holiday. But all the hustle can easily crowd out the holy. We find ourselves so busy preparing for Christmas that we miss Christ Himself. What if simplicity is not about subtraction, but about focus? Not emptiness, but fullness of the right things?

Micah 6:8 reminds us that God doesn't measure our worth by our busyness or brilliance. He's not impressed by noise or production. He calls us to act justly, love mercy, and walk humbly with Him. These are quiet acts, small choices, faithful steps. Simplicity is a return to those basics. It's choosing stillness over speed, intention over obligation, depth over decoration.

This Advent, what might it look like to rediscover the sacred in the simple? Maybe it's turning off your phone during dinner, lighting a candle and sitting in silence, or saying no to one more event so you can say yes to rest. Maybe it's whispering a short prayer in the morning before anything else.

Simplicity doesn't mean doing less just for the sake of it—it means making space for what matters most: God's presence, people you love, and a soul at peace.

Prayer

Lord, simplify my heart. Strip away distractions. Let this season be filled with what truly matters—Your presence and Your love. Amen.

Today's Journaling Prompt

Take a quiet moment today to reflect on one area of your life that feels cluttered or distracting. What would it look like to clear away the noise so you have room for what truly matters? Write down the things you need to say "no" to, and then make a list of the things you long to say "yes" to but haven't had the time or space for. As you journal, consider how choosing simplicity can open your heart to God's presence in a deeper way this Christmas season.

REDISCOVER SILENCE

Scripture

Be still, and know that I am God; I will be exalted among the nations, I will be exalted in the earth.
- Psalm 46:10

Reflection

Day

9

*W*e live in a world that fears silence. We fill every gap with noise—music in the background, scrolling through our phones, podcasts while we drive. Even when we're alone, our thoughts are loud. Silence feels uncomfortable, maybe even awkward. But in Scripture, silence is not emptiness—it's expectancy. It's often the quiet before God moves.

Think back to the very first Christmas. Before angels sang in the sky, there was stillness in the fields. Before Jesus took His first breath, the world held its own. In that hushed moment, Heaven touched Earth.

God doesn't always shout to get our attention. Sometimes, He whispers, and sometimes, He waits for us to get quiet enough to hear Him. Psalm 46:10 is not just an invitation—it's a command: *Be still.* Stop striving. Cease speaking. Let the world turn without your input for a moment. In that stillness, we begin to know—not just in our minds, but deep in our hearts—that He is God.

Advent invites us to slow down, not speed up. It's not about how much we can do but how well we can listen. Silence becomes a spiritual practice—not an absence of sound, but a posture of surrender. It trains us to hear again. To recognize the gentle nudge of God's Spirit and to receive rather than perform.

The most powerful thing you can do today is to turn everything off. Sit in the quiet. Take a deep breath. Wait on the Lord. The world will clamor for your attention again soon enough. But for now—just listen. You may be surprised by what you hear in the silence.

Prayer

God, teach me to be still. Quiet my heart, my mind, my surroundings. Help me rediscover You in the silence. Amen.

Today's Journaling Prompt

Read Psalm 139:23-24. Set a timer for five minutes today. Sit in silence with no distractions. Simply be. Let God meet you there. Journal what came to your mind during this time of reflection.

REDISCOVER GENEROSITY

Day

Scripture

In everything I did, I showed you that by this kind of hard work we must help the weak, remembering the words the Lord Jesus himself said: 'It is more blessed to give than to receive.
- Acts 20:35

10

Reflection

*T*he Christmas story is one of extravagant, soul-deep generosity. God gave His only Son—not because humanity deserved it, but because love compelled it. Mary gave her future. Joseph gave his security. The shepherds gave their voice. The Magi gave their finest gifts. And Jesus gave Himself.

This kind of generosity isn't defined by wealth or possessions. It's characterized by willingness. It doesn't wait for the perfect moment or a padded bank account. It starts with a heart that sees others and says, "How can I love them well today?"

In our world, especially during the holiday season, consumerism often drowns out compassion. We're told to buy more, get more, and want more. But the quiet power of giving—true, intentional giving—can cut through that noise and speak directly to the soul. Generosity reminds us of what truly matters.

And the beauty of it? Generosity comes in many forms. A phone call to someone who's lonely. A warm meal given to a struggling neighbor. Time spent with a grieving friend. A word of encouragement written in a card. **These moments may seem small, but in God's economy, nothing given in love is wasted.**

When we give, we echo the heartbeat of Heaven. We become part of the redemptive story God is still telling. So today, ask not, "What do I *have* to give?" but "How can I reflect the generosity of Jesus?" In doing so, you'll find something unexpected: your own heart expanding with joy, meaning, and purpose.

Because it truly is more blessed to give than to receive.

Prayer

Father, thank You for giving so generously. Help me reflect Your heart through how I give. May my generosity bring joy to others and glory to You. Amen.

Today's Journaling Prompt

Write down at least one small meaningful way to give today to someone specific—money, time, help, or encouragement. Complete the act of generosity this week, not looking for applause or accolades. Let it be an act of worship.

REDISCOVER OBEDIENCE

Scripture

**When Joseph woke up, he did what the angel of the Lord had commanded him and took Mary home as his wife.
- Matthew 1:24**

Day

11

Reflection

*O*bedience is often unspectacular. It's not flashy. It doesn't make headlines. And yet, it is one of the most profound expressions of trust. Joseph's story proves that.

He wasn't a prophet or a preacher. He didn't write a gospel or lead crowds. He was a humble carpenter, engaged to a young woman who was suddenly—and scandalously—pregnant. Every logical reason said to walk away quietly. But when God spoke, Joseph listened. Then, he acted.

There's no record of him arguing with the angel. No list of questions. No bargaining. Just obedience. He woke up and did what God asked. He stood beside Mary. He stepped into a story bigger than his own. And he helped raise the Savior of the world.

We often think obedience must be grand—quitting jobs, selling homes, moving across oceans. **But most of the time, obedience looks like faithfulness in the ordinary.** Choosing kindness instead of retaliation. Holding our tongues when we want to speak harshly. Saying yes to God's whisper when it's easier to say no.

Joseph didn't need all the details to obey. He just needed to trust the One who gave the command. And in doing so, he became a quiet hero in God's redemption story. You can, too.

This Christmas, what is God asking of you? Maybe it's a step that scares you. Perhaps it's a sacrifice no one else sees. **Obedience may not always make sense—but it always makes a difference.**

Prayer

Father, help me to obey You—not out of fear, but out of love. Give me the courage to say yes when it's hard and to trust You even when I don't understand. Amen.

Today's Journaling Prompt

What is one area in your life where God might be asking you to obey? Write a prayer of surrender asking for strength, courage, and wisdom to follow through.

REDISCOVER PURPOSE

Scripture

And we know that in all things God works for the good of those who love him, who have been called according to his purpose.
- Romans 8:28

Day

12

Reflection

*P*urpose isn't always loud or obvious. It doesn't always come with a clear sign or a voice from Heaven. Sometimes, it looks like a journey you didn't plan—like a census that uproots your life. That was the case for Mary and Joseph. A government order sent them on a long, tiring journey to Bethlehem—at the worst possible time. But God was in it and was fulfilling ancient promises through inconvenient circumstances.

That's the mystery of God's purpose. It rarely feels dramatic in real-time. More often, it's disguised in the ordinary. In a daily commute. A conversation over dinner. A small act of kindness. A job you're not even sure you're passionate about. And yet, God is weaving those threads into something eternal.

Maybe today doesn't feel significant. Maybe you're wrestling with routine or restlessness, but don't miss the holy that hides in your here and now. God doesn't waste a single moment. He is forming Christ in you. He is planting seeds of influence through your consistency, your attitude, and your surrender.

Even your pain has a purpose. When life feels confusing, God is still working—not just to fix things, but to form you. To stretch your trust. To prepare you for things unseen. One day, you may look back and see how it all connected. For now, hold onto the promise: He is working all things—yes, even this—for your good and His glory.

Prayer

Lord, help me to trust that my life has purpose—even when I can't see it. Use my ordinary for Your glory. Teach me to walk in faith, knowing You are at work in all things. Amen.

Today's Journaling Prompt

Reflect on *three* "ordinary" parts of your day. How might God be using that space, habit, or routine to grow your character or bless someone else?

REDISCOVER TRUST

Scripture

**Trust in the Lord with all your heart and lean not on your own understanding; in all your ways submit to him, and he will make your paths straight.
- Proverbs 3:5–6**

Day

13

Reflection

*T*rust is the foundation of every deep and lasting relationship. But trusting God—completely, fully, with your whole heart—is not something that comes naturally. Especially when life feels uncertain, painful, or unpredictable. When circumstances don't make sense, our instincts often lean toward control. We want answers. We want a plan. We want to see what's ahead before we take the next step.

But Proverbs 3:5-6 invites us into something deeper. It calls us to lay down our desire for clarity and pick up the posture of surrender. It challenges us to trust God not just with part of our heart, but with *all* of it. To lean not on what we understand, but on who God is—God's faithfulness, God's goodness, and God's sovereignty.

Mary, a young woman with her own hopes and dreams, was told she would carry the Son of God. Her future changed in an instant. She had every reason to panic, every reason to question. And yet her response was one of trust: *"Let it be to me according to your word."* That kind of faith doesn't come from having all the answers. It comes from knowing and trusting the One who holds them.

Trust is not the absence of fear—it's the choice to move forward despite fear. It's saying, "God, I don't know what You're doing, but I know You and that's enough." It's choosing to believe that God is weaving something beautiful, even when all you see are tangled threads.

This Advent season, you may face situations that don't make sense. You might carry questions, disappointments, or delays. But even then—especially then—God is inviting you to trust Him. Not because you see the whole picture, but because He does. And He's already gone ahead of you, preparing the way.

Prayer

God, when I don't understand, help me trust You more. Strengthen my faith. Draw me closer. Let my life be anchored in Your promises, not my circumstances. Let it be to me according to your word. Amen.

Today's Journaling Prompt

Which area of your life feels unclear or out of your control right now? Write honestly about your fears, questions, or doubts. Then reflect: what would it look like to surrender those to God today? After spending time reflecting, list the areas where God has been faithful in the past. Remember this: The God who proved faithful in the past will not fail you in the future—trust His unchanging hand.

REDISCOVER SERVING

Scripture

**For even the Son of Man did not come to be served, but to serve, and to give his life as a ransom for many.
- Mark 10:45**

Day

14

Reflection

*J*oy and service may not seem like natural companions. In a world that often tells us to prioritize self-care, chase success, and look out for number one, the idea of pouring ourselves out for others can feel like a burden. But Jesus flips the script. He didn't come to be served, though He was the King of Kings. He came to serve, and in doing so, He revealed the unexpected truth: **real joy is found not in being elevated, but in love, in meeting others where they are.**

Serving isn't always spotlight-worthy. It often goes unnoticed and uncelebrated. It looks like wiping counters, holding babies, listening patiently, or giving up your schedule to meet someone else's need. Yet it is in these quiet acts of love that something sacred happens: our hearts begin to mirror the heart of Christ.

Joy in serving doesn't come from applause or recognition. It comes from knowing you are part of something eternal— bringing light, hope, and healing into someone else's world. It shifts your focus from self to others and aligns your life with the mission of Jesus.

You don't need a platform or a program to serve. Start where you are. Look for the unnoticed and unmet needs in your home, workplace, community, or church. Ask God to show you where to step in, because when you serve with humility and love, you experience a joy the world can't manufacture—a joy that runs deep and lasts long.

Prayer

Lord, make me a servant like You. Open my eyes to the needs around me. Help me love people not just with words, but with action. Let joy rise as I serve in Your name. Amen.

Today's Journaling Prompt

Think about a recent opportunity you served someone—big or small. How did it impact you? How might God be inviting you to serve joyfully in this Advent season? Write about one person or place where you feel called to serve, and what steps you can take this week to show up with a servant's heart.

REDISCOVER LIGHT

Scripture

**The light shines in the darkness, and the darkness has not overcome it
- John 1:5**

Reflection

$\mathscr{T}$he world often feels wrapped in shadow. From the heaviness of global unrest to the quiet pain of personal struggle, darkness can feel overwhelming. Fear creeps in. Hope flickers. Questions arise. But Christmas proclaims a powerful truth that pushes back the night: **the Light has come, and the darkness cannot overcome it**.

This isn't just poetry—it's a promise. Jesus stepped into a dark and broken world to bring light that the night could never extinguish. From the first words of creation—*"Let there*

Day

15

be light"—to the birth of Christ in Bethlehem, God has always been in the business of overcoming darkness. His light is not fragile. It does not fade. It stands firm and shines through even the thickest shadow.

In the middle of grief, confusion, or silence, His light still breaks through. He brings hope to the hopeless, comfort to the weary, and clarity when everything feels uncertain. Even when your path is dimly lit, He is still there—guiding, revealing, and illuminating your next step.

You don't have to have it all figured out. You don't need to be fearless or strong. Just look to the Light. Let it shine into the corners of your doubt, fear, and exhaustion. Let it remind you that the story is not over—and that Light has the final word.

This Advent, choose to rediscover the Light. Not just as a theme, but as a Person—Jesus Christ, the Light of the world. His light still shines. And the darkness still cannot win.

Prayer

Light a candle and sit quietly for a few moments. Then pray, "Jesus, You are the Light I need. Shine in my heart. Chase away the darkness and the shadows. Help me see You clearly and follow You fully. Amen."

Today's Journaling Prompt

Where in your life are you feeling the weight of darkness—whether through fear, grief, uncertainty, or weariness? Take a moment to write honestly about that place. Then reflect: how has God's light shown up for you in past seasons of struggle? What would it look like to invite His light into this area now? Get into prayer and ask God to shine His hope and truth into the places that feel dim.

REDISCOVER WORSHIP

Scripture

And Mary said: "My soul glorifies the Lord and my spirit rejoices in God my Savior"
- Luke 1:46–47

Day

16

Reflection

*W*hen Mary received the life-altering news that she would carry the Messiah, her response wasn't fear, complaint, or control—it was worship. Her song, known as the *Magnificat*, flowed not from comfort or clarity, but from a heart grounded in trust. *"My soul glorifies the Lord, and my spirit rejoices in God my Savior."* These words weren't shallow or sentimental. They rose from a young woman whose world had just been turned upside down.

Worship isn't about having all the answers. It's about surrendering to the One who does.

For Mary, worship didn't erase the uncertainty ahead—it simply anchored her to God in the midst of it. Her reputation would be questioned. Her path would be difficult. And yet, she magnified the Lord.

True worship is more than singing songs on Sunday—it's a posture of the heart. It happens in quiet moments, in whispered prayers, in lifting our eyes even when life is heavy. It's choosing to praise even when things don't make sense. It's remembering that God is still worthy—always.

In a season full of noise, activity, and distraction, rediscovering worship means slowing down and turning our attention upward. **Not because life is perfect, but because He is.** Worship recenters us. It reminds us of God's greatness and goodness. It opens our hearts to His presence and gives space for joy—even in uncertainty.

Let this Advent be a time where you don't just hear holiday music, but you respond with worship. Let your soul magnify the Lord.

Prayer

Lord, give me a heart like Mary's—a heart that worships even when the way is unclear. Let my soul magnify You. Fill my spirit with praise. Amen.

Today's Journaling Prompt

Read Luke 1:46-55. Then, write your own *Magnificat*—a personal song or prayer of praise for who God is and what He has done in your life.

REDISCOVER PEACE

Day

Scripture

For to us a child is born, to us a son is given, and the government will be on his shoulders. And he will be called Wonderful Counselor, Mighty God, Everlasting Father, Prince of Peace.
- Isaiah 9:6

17

Reflection

*O*ne of the most comforting titles given to Jesus is "Prince of Peace." It's not just a poetic name—it's a powerful declaration. In a world marked by division, uncertainty, anxiety, and noise, peace often feels out of reach. We search for it in quiet moments, in fixed schedules, in financial security, or in stable relationships. **But true peace doesn't come from everything falling into place. It comes from Jesus Himself.**

The night Jesus was born, the angels proclaimed, *"peace on earth"*—not because the world was calm, but because **Peace had come**. Christ entered our chaos, not to escape it, but to redeem it. That's what real peace is: not the absence of problems, but the presence of a Person who holds us steady through them.

Where in your life do you feel anxious, burdened, or out of control? Jesus isn't distant from those places. He steps right into them. He doesn't wait for us to clean up the mess—He brings peace into the middle of it. The same Savior who calmed the storm with a word can calm your anxious heart today.

Isaiah reminds us that *"the government will be on His shoulders."* That means your life, your worries, your future—they're not on your shoulders anymore. They're on His. You don't carry it alone.

This Advent season, don't just long for peace—invite the Prince of Peace to reign in every corner of your life. Let Him quiet your mind, calm your fears, and bring rest to your soul. He is still the Peace your heart is longing for.

Prayer

Jesus, You are my peace. When the world around me feels loud and unsure, help me lean into You. Calm my thoughts. Center my heart. Rule in me today. Amen.

Today's Journaling Prompt

Identify one area of your life that feels anxious or chaotic. Write a prayer, poem, or worship song, or draw a picture of Jesus' peace being there.

REDISCOVER COMMUNITY

Day

Scripture

Every day they continued to meet together in the temple courts. They broke bread in their homes and ate together with glad and sincere hearts. - Acts 2:46

18

Reflection

*C*hristmas draws people together—around tables, trees, and treasured traditions. But community is more than being in the same room; it's about being truly seen and known. The early church embodied this kind of connection. They didn't just meet once a week or exchange surface-level greetings. They *shared life*.

They gathered in the temple courts, yes—but also in each other's homes. They ate together. They prayed together. They laughed, cried, learned, and grew together. There was no pretending, no performance—just a sincere desire to walk through life with one another under the grace of Christ.

That's the kind of community our hearts long for. And it's the kind of community Jesus modeled. He surrounded Himself with imperfect people. He washed their feet. He listened to their hearts. He invested in their stories. In a season that can feel overwhelming or isolating, Jesus gently invites us back into connection—not just with Him, but with others.

Maybe you feel lonely this Christmas, or perhaps you're surrounded by people but still feel disconnected. The truth is, we all hunger for belonging, and we all have something to offer. Community isn't about having a perfect home or being the ideal host—it's about showing up, heart open, arms extended.

This Advent, rediscover the gift of community. Invite someone over for coffee. Text a friend you've been thinking about. Go to church. Join a small group or reach out to someone who might be struggling. Open your door and open your life.

You don't need to fix anyone. Just be present. That alone can be a sacred offering.

Prayer

God, thank You for the gift of community. Help me invest in relationships that reflect Your love. Teach me to give and receive encouragement and grace. Amen.

Today's Journaling Prompt

Don't wait for connection. Create it. Ask God to reveal the name of someone to write a text, make a call, or schedule a coffee. Journal how it felt afterward—was it life-giving, stretching, or surprising? Let God use your presence to create belonging.

REDISCOVER THE UNEXPECTED

Day 19

Scripture

But the angel said to them, "Do not be afraid. I bring you good news that will cause great joy for all the people. Today in the town of David, a Savior has been born to you; he is the Messiah, the Lord.
- Luke 2:10–11

Reflection

The first Christmas shattered expectations. No royal announcement. No lavish celebration. Instead, a teenage girl gave birth in a stable. A feeding trough cradled the Messiah. Shepherds—blue-collar, overlooked men. These were the first to hear the news. **Heaven broke into Earth in a place no one thought to look.**

This isn't just a charming story; it's a pattern. God has always worked through the unexpected. He chose Moses, a fugitive with a stutter, to speak to Pharaoh. He picked David, a shepherd boy, to be king. **And He used a crucified Savior to bring salvation to the world.**

Maybe this year hasn't gone the way you imagined. Maybe your plans have unraveled or taken a direction you didn't see coming. If so, you're standing on holy ground. **The very detours that frustrate us can be the spaces where God breaks through.**

The shepherds didn't go looking for angels. They were just doing their jobs—watching sheep in the cold night. But the unexpected interrupted their routine with glory, and when they followed the message, they saw Jesus with their own eyes.

The unexpected invites us to stop and listen. It stretches our faith. It pushes us to ask, "What might God be doing here?" Instead of resisting it, we can choose to wonder. We can look for Jesus even in our confusion.

This Advent, may you welcome the unexpected—not as a threat to your plans, but as an invitation to God's presence. The story unfolding in your life may not be what you envisioned, but it may be exactly what your heart needs.

Prayer

Lord, help me embrace the unexpected with open hands and a soft heart. Use it to grow my trust and deepen my joy in You. Amen.

Today's Journaling Prompt

Step 1: Reflect - Draw a simple timeline of this past year. Highlight 3–5 key moments where things didn't go as expected—these could be disappointments, surprises, interruptions, or changes in direction. Beside each one, jot a few words describing how you felt in that moment (e.g., "frustrated," "lost," "confused," "hopeful," etc.).

Rediscover the Unexpected

Step 2: Reframe - Now, revisit each of those moments. Underneath each, write what *God might have been doing* in that season. Even if it's still unclear, write a sentence that begins with:

- *"Maybe God was teaching me…"*
- *"Maybe God was protecting me from…"*
- *"Maybe God was preparing me for…"*

Step 3: Respond - Write a short letter to God titled *"Thank You for the Unexpected."* In it, thank Him for at least one moment on your timeline. Be honest about how it felt and what you're still learning. Then, express your desire to trust Him more, even when the way ahead feels uncertain.

REDISCOVER HEALING

Scripture

He was despised and rejected by mankind, a man of suffering, and familiar with pain. Like one from whom people hide their faces he was despised, and we held him in low esteem.
- Isaiah 53:3

Day

20

Reflection

"By His wounds we are healed." These words from Isaiah 53:5 go far beyond physical ailments. They speak to a deeper need—the healing of our hearts, our past, our souls. Jesus didn't come merely to relieve symptoms; He came to restore what was broken at the core of who we are.

This world leaves its mark—rejection, loss, betrayal, and disappointment. Many carry wounds hidden behind smiles and festive greetings. The holidays often magnify what's missing—whether it's a person, a dream, or a sense of peace. Pain has a way of lingering in the quiet corners of our hearts.

But Isaiah reminds us that Jesus understands. **He is not a distant Savior unfamiliar with suffering.** He *is* the Man of Sorrows. He walked through loneliness, was misunderstood, betrayed, beaten, and crucified. Why? So that you could be made whole.

Healing isn't always instant. Sometimes, God mends us slowly—layer by layer, over time. It can feel like winter light rising slowly over a frozen field—soft, almost imperceptible at first. But it comes because Christ came. **He steps into our broken world, takes on our pain, and invites us to lay our wounds at His feet.**

This Advent, rediscover healing—not just from what has happened to you, but for who you are becoming in Christ. His wounds are not just a symbol of suffering; they are a gateway to your restoration.

Let this be the season you stop pretending you're okay—and start letting Jesus tend to what's hurting.

Don't push away your pain—bring it to the manger. Let Jesus meet you there. Let Him speak peace over your unrest and hope over your hurt.

Prayer

Lord, I bring You my pain today. Heal what's broken in me. Make me whole in ways I don't even fully understand. Thank You for coming to carry my wounds. Amen.

Today's Journaling Prompt

Write a letter to Jesus expressing your hurt. Invite Him into those places where you need healing. Write Scriptural promises as a reminder of God's goodness. Below are three examples:

Rediscover Healing

Hurt: *"Lord, I feel abandoned and alone."*
Scriptural Promise: *"Never will I leave you; never will I forsake you."* (Hebrews 13:5)

Hurt: *"I feel anxious and overwhelmed by everything around me."*
Scriptural Promise: *"Cast all your anxiety on him because he cares for you."* (1 Peter 5:7)

Hurt: *"God, I feel like I've failed too many times."*
Scriptural Promise: *"His mercies are new every morning; great is your faithfulness."* (Lamentations 3:23)

REDISCOVER PATIENCE

Scripture

**But the fruit of the Spirit is love, joy, peace, forbearance, kindness, goodness, faithfulness...
- Galatians 5:22**

Day

21

Reflection

*P*atience is one of those virtues we deeply appreciate in others but often struggle to practice ourselves. It doesn't come naturally in a world of instant everything. Yet, patience—also translated as *forbearance*—is a fruit of the Spirit, a visible sign of God's presence and maturity in us.

Advent is, at its core, a season of waiting. We remember Israel's long wait for the Messiah. We reflect on Mary's months of carrying the hope for the world in her womb. And we live in the now-but-not-yet tension, waiting for Christ's return and for His presence to break through in our daily lives.

Waiting is never easy. It can feel like silence and give us the feeling of being forgotten. But Scripture reminds us that God is never slow in keeping His promises (2 Peter 3:9). God is not absent in our waiting—God is *active*. He is preparing, aligning, refining, and transforming us while we wait.

Mary's story teaches us that patience doesn't mean passivity. It means trust. She waited with faith, carrying a promise she couldn't fully understand. You may be in a season where you're waiting for healing, reconciliation, provision, or purpose. Know this: **God is at work in the waiting.**

Patience grows when we release our timelines and trust in His plan, and when we believe that the waiting isn't wasted but is fertile ground for spiritual growth. Sometimes, the most powerful things God does in us happen not after the waiting, but *through* it.

This Advent, rediscover patience. Let the slow work of God deepen your faith and shape your soul.

Prayer

God, grow patience in me. Teach me to wait well—with hope, with trust, and with peace. Help me surrender my need for control and rest in Your perfect timing. Amen.

Today's Journaling Prompt

Write a short letter to God, surrendering your timeline. Then, choose one small daily practice to embrace waiting with grace this week—like turning off your phone when standing in line or starting your day with a silent prayer. Set a reminder on your phone and, later today, journal how that practice shifts your perspective on waiting.

REDISCOVER FREEDOM

Day 22

Scripture

So if the Son sets you free, you will be free indeed.
- John 8:36

Reflection

Christmas tells the story of our liberation. It's not just about a baby born in Bethlehem—it's about a Savior who came to rescue us. Jesus didn't enter our world to decorate it with peace and nostalgia. He came to break chains. To set captives free. To speak life where shame and fear had ruled.

And yet, many of us still live bound. We carry guilt that Christ already bore. We allow shame to shape our identity. We strive to earn love and approval that God has already lavished upon us. We live guarded—afraid of failure, clinging to control, unsure of grace.

But Jesus came to change that.

Freedom in Christ isn't the absence of struggle—it's the presence of truth. It's knowing that your worth doesn't fluctuate with your performance, that your past doesn't disqualify your future. It means that fear doesn't get the final say. Jesus sets us free not just from what holds us back, but for a new kind of life: one marked by joy, rest, and wholeness.

This Advent, rediscover the freedom that is already yours in Christ. Breathe it in. Let it seep into the hidden corners of your soul. Let go of the weight you were never meant to carry.

You don't have to strive to be enough. In Jesus, you already are.

Prayer

Jesus, thank You for setting me free. Help me walk in that freedom. Remind me I don't have to earn what You've already given. Amen.

Today's Journaling Prompt

Is there an area where you're living like you're still in chains? Write it down. Then, write "FREE" over it in bold letters.

REDISCOVER PRIORITIES

Scripture

**But seek first his kingdom
and his righteousness,
and all these things will be
given to you as well."
- Matthew 6:33**

Day

23

Reflection

*A*dvent invites us to reflect on the greatest priority: seeking God first. Amid the festivities, the food, the gifts, and the gatherings, it's easy to let our attention drift. We may become so caught up in the seasonal hustle and bustle that we forget what Christmas is really about—God's invitation to draw near to Him and to make His kingdom our first priority.

Jesus knew how easy it was to get distracted by the demands of life, the worries of the world, and the pursuit of things that, in the end, don't last. He reminds us in Matthew 6 that when we seek Him above all else, everything else falls into place. When we prioritize God's kingdom, our hearts align with His will, and we experience peace—not because everything is perfect, but because we trust that God holds it all in His hands.

As the Advent season soon comes to a close, consider where your priorities have been. Has Christmas, with all its good things, crowded out the time and space for the best thing—an intimate relationship with Jesus?

It's easy to look at our calendars and feel overwhelmed, but the truth is that our hearts will always follow what we put first. If we seek Jesus first, the joy, peace, and love of His presence will fill every corner of our lives—more than any gift or experience ever could.

Priorities aren't just about what we choose to do—they are about who we choose to be. Who are you becoming through the choices you're making? Is your heart set on the things that truly matter, or are you chasing temporary distractions?

This Christmas, make room for Jesus. Start with Him, and everything else will follow.

Prayer

Lord, thank You for reminding me that You are the true gift of this season. Help me realign my priorities with Yours. Let me seek You first in everything—trusting that when I do, You will take care of the rest. Amen.

Today's Journaling Prompt

Step 1: Reevaluate
Write down three things you've given priority to recently. Next to each one, ask yourself: "How does this align with God's kingdom? Does it bring me closer to His heart, or does it pull me away?"

Step 2: Reset

Choose one area where you feel called to shift your priority. It might be making time for prayer, serving others, or simplifying your schedule. Write a simple action plan to start placing God at the center of that area.

REDISCOVER COMPASSION

Day

Scripture

Therefore, as God's chosen people, holy and dearly loved, clothe yourselves with compassion, kindness, humility, gentleness and patience.
- Colossians 3:12

24

Reflection

"Clothe yourselves with compassion…" This simple yet powerful command from Colossians reminds us that compassion isn't just something we feel—it's something we choose to wear, day in and day out. It's a posture of the heart, a decision to look beyond our own busy lives and extend grace to the people around us.

In the whirlwind of the holiday season, it's easy to become wrapped up in the rush of shopping, events, and the endless to-do lists. We can become impatient, distracted, and sometimes even indifferent to the needs of those around us. But Advent, at its core, calls us to slow down and recalibrate our hearts. It invites us to take the time to see others—not as obstacles to our plans, but as fellow image-bearers of God, each with their own joys and struggles.

Jesus demonstrated compassion throughout His life. When He saw the crowds, He didn't just notice them—He was moved by them. His heart broke for the suffering, the lonely, and the lost. Jesus acted on that compassion, meeting needs and offering grace. He didn't stay distant—He came near.

This Advent, as we reflect on the birth of Christ, let's also rediscover His heart for others. Compassion isn't always about grand gestures. Sometimes it's as simple as a kind word, a listening ear, or an act of service. Every small act of compassion reflects the love of Christ and brings us closer to the heart of the season.

Prayer

Lord, give me eyes to see and a heart to care. Help me clothe myself in compassion, just as You are compassionate with me. Amen.

Today's Journaling Prompt

What is one small way you can extend compassion to someone today? It could be a simple word of encouragement, a small act of kindness, or offering your time to listen. Write down the specific actions you will take, then reflect on how it went and how it made you feel.

CHRISTMAS EVE: REDISCOVER THE STORY

Day

Scripture

The Word became flesh and made his dwelling among us. We have seen his glory, the glory of the one and only Son, who came from the Father, full of grace and truth. - John 1:14

25

Reflection

"*The Word became flesh and made His dwelling among us…*" This verse from John 1:14 is not just a poetic description of a distant historical event. It is the culmination of God's long pursuit of His people. This is where Heaven and Earth meet—where the Creator of the universe chooses to dwell in the very creation He made. Love made tangible. God becomes human, and in doing so, touches every aspect of humanity with grace and truth.

At the heart of Christmas lies the reality that God has not left us alone. He has not remained distant in His perfection but has entered into our mess. He walked among us, felt our pain, celebrated our joys, and ultimately gave Himself for us. This moment of divine intervention in history is not just something to recall in December; it's a living, breathing reality that continues to unfold in our lives. The birth of Christ is not merely a historical event—it is an invitation to live differently, to live as witnesses of that glory, and to carry His love forward.

On this Christmas Eve, let's reflect on how this truth has reshaped our own lives. How has God's love changed your life? How has His presence transformed your relationships, your choices, and your purpose? Where in your journey has His grace written over your brokenness?

Don't let the significance of this season fade once the wrapping paper is gone. **Christmas should never truly end, because the story of Christ's birth is the story of His ongoing presence in our lives.** Let it shape us, move us, and send us forward—until He returns.

Prayer

Jesus, thank You for writing me into Your story. Help me carry it with joy and live it with purpose. Let others see You in me. Amen.

Today's Journaling Prompt

Take time to write your own Advent reflection. Over these past 25 days, where have you seen God meet you? What has been revealed in your heart? What have you learned? In what ways have you experienced God's healing, or what new longings and stirrings has God awakened within you?

CHRISTMAS DAY: REDISCOVER CHRIST

Day

26

Scripture

**The Son is the image of the invisible God, the firstborn over all creation For in him all things were created: things in heaven and on earth, visible and invisible, whether thrones or powers or rulers or authorities; all things have been created through him and for him. He is before all things, and in him all things hold together.
- Colossians 1:15–17**

Reflection

*T*oday is Christmas—the day we celebrate the greatest gift ever given: Christ, the Savior of the world! While this day is filled with gifts, laughter, festive meals, and cherished traditions, let's remember that the heart of Christmas is Christ Himself. In Colossians 1:15-17, we are reminded that Jesus is the image of the invisible God, the Creator wrapped in human flesh. The eternal, limitless One chose to enter our world, to step into time and space, to be with us.

It's easy, in the hustle and bustle of this season, to get caught up in the externals—decorations, family gatherings, and even the routines of our faith traditions. But let's take a moment to truly center ourselves on Christ, the source of all these blessings. **Jesus is not just a part of Christmas; He *is* Christmas.** He is the reason for everything we celebrate today.

As you reflect on the manger today—in your heart—let yourself reflect on the beauty and the weight of this moment. Picture the scene: the quiet of the night, the humble surroundings, the scent of the straw, the vulnerability of God made flesh, the scandalous reality that the Creator of the universe would come as a helpless baby.

This isn't just a historical event to admire from a distance; it's a living, breathing reality that impacts us every day. As we celebrate, let's *rediscover* Christ—not just as a story or a symbol, but as the very center of our lives. Let Him be the peace that calms our hearts, the joy that fills our spirits, and the reason we have hope, even in the most trying times.

Prayer

Jesus, You are the center of it all. On this Christmas Day, I pause to remember that every gift, every song, every celebration points back to You. Thank You for leaving heaven to step into our world, for holding all things together—including my life. Help me to rediscover You, not just today, but every day. Let my heart overflow with gratitude, joy, and worship as I keep You at the center of my story. Amen.

Today's Journaling Prompt

Today, intentionally share the love of Christ with someone around you—whether through a word of encouragement, a kind gesture, or simply sharing the truth of who He is. Make today about more than just the gifts you receive or give; make it about reflecting the heart of Christ to others.

A Special Thank You

I want to offer a heartfelt thank you to each of you who has joined in this Advent journey through *Rediscovering Christmas*. I know that for many, this season can feel overwhelming, filled with commitments and responsibilities. But the fact that you have made space to reflect on the deeper meaning of Christmas speaks volumes about your desire to grow in faith and connection with Christ.

By choosing to engage with this devotional, you have intentionally set aside time to reflect, to pray, to ponder, and to rediscover what makes this season so extraordinary—the presence of Christ in our midst. It's not easy to slow down in a world that constantly pulls us in a thousand directions. Still, your commitment to this practice is a powerful reminder that the heart of Christmas isn't found in the flurry of activity, but in the stillness of recognizing Christ as Emmanuel—God with us.

Whether this is your first Advent season spent intentionally reflecting on the meaning of Christmas or you've walked through many seasons of waiting and preparing, I want to honor your faithfulness. Your journey is meaningful, and I am truly grateful for the way you've allowed this time of Advent to draw you closer to Jesus.

Rediscover Christmas

I pray that you continue to rediscover the wonder of Christmas today and into the new year. May God's presence fill your heart with peace, joy, and unshakable hope. Thank you for making this season of Advent a time of deeper reflection and for choosing to keep Christ at the center of it all.

May you carry the light of His love throughout this year and beyond, and may your life reflect the grace and beauty of the Savior who was born to redeem us all. - Nathan